LOVE, LEAD, SERVE

ANTHONY F. RUSSO

LOVE, LEAD, SERVE

the christian man's call to
serve his family and his church

Love, Lead, Serve
The Christian Man's Call to Serve His
Family and His Church
Copyright © 2023 by Anthony F. Russo

ISBN: 978-0-9982445-5-6

Cover Design and typeset by
www.greatwriting.org
Printed in the United States of America

Published by Broken Road Books
www.GraceAndPeaceRadio.com
www.LoveLeadServeBook.com
For bulk order pricing,
please contact us at
bulk@LoveLeadServeBook.com

BROKEN ROAD BOOKS

"So I sought for a man among them who would make a wall, and stand in the gap before Me on behalf of the land. . ."
Ezekiel 22:30

Dedicated to Christian Men Everywhere:

May you be the man standing in the gap before the Lord.

Part 1

Your Private Life as a Christian Man

1. Prioritize Prayer and the Scriptures

2. Trust God in Trials and Suffering

3. Be Alert Against the Enemy

4. Always Be Ready

Part 2

Your Marriage and Your Home

1. Know the Sanctifying Power of Your Home

2. Practice Love and Good Works at Home

3. Model Christ in Your Home

4. Lead with a Christlike Attitude

Part 3

Your Ministry

1. Practice Loving Discretion

2. Don't Neglect your Family for Ministry

3. Take Control of Your Time and Your Commitments

4. Get Wisdom for Life-Changing Decisions

Contents

You Must Withstand and Stand

"Therefore take up the whole armor of God, that you may be able to withstand in the evil day, and having done all, to stand. . ."
(Ephesians 6:13)

In Paul's letter to the Ephesians he directs a few of his remarks to different groups of Christians, knowing his letter would be read aloud to all the believers there. He writes to wives, to husbands, to masters, and even includes a few words for the children and for slaves.

But in this verse, Paul is addressing *all* Christians. Paul is telling every Christian to put on the whole armor of God for two main purposes: to withstand and to stand. Those early Christians needed the armor of God so they could withstand and stand, and so do we today. And since the Lord has called men to lead in the home and in the church, we are the ones who must take the lead in this charge.

Withstand in the Evil Day

God's Word tells us that we live in evil days. The kings of the world and its rulers continue to take counsel together against the Lord and His Christ (Psalm 2). The Bible also warns us that we live in the last days (1 John 2:18). Every day the news headlines show the trajectory of this world. It continues in sin as Judgment Day draws closer.

At the same time, men of this world have lost their courage. They have taken the bribe the culture offers them. They laid down their weapons and surrendered in exchange for comfortable lives. Men have compromised on their convictions and chosen entertainment and ease rather than doing the hard and necessary things we are called to. And, tragically, many of these men are right in our own churches.

This world needs men who courageously take their stand against the culture. But courage is not enough. What good is it for a man to stand against the many evils in this world, but still not be born again? What good is bravery against tyrants without the indwelling Christ and the power of the Holy

Spirit? Standing against the evils of the world is good and right, but it is far more important to take a stand in the Name of Jesus Christ, and for His glory.

We need men like Noah and Lot. Peter commends both men for their bold stand for the Lord. Noah preached salvation to his ungodly generation and "righteous Lot. . . that righteous man. . . tormented his righteous soul from day to day" as he watched the wickedness of Sodom and Gomorrah in his generation (2 Peter 2:4-8). These men lived among godless people who did wicked things, yet they stood fast and proclaimed the Name of the Lord.

We must be men who
withstand in the evil day.

Stand for Christ

Noah and Lot lived before the time of Christ, but they stood for Christ. They preached Christ.

A man is never truly a man until he is God's man. The man who stands for Christ when everything is against him, that man is unstoppable. He has been battle tested. Such a man has become a warrior of the Lord. His hands are trained for war (Psalm 18:34). He knows how to break through the enemy's defenses and can climb over a wall (Psalm 18:29). Like David and Samson, when the lions and bears of this world attack, he grabs them and tears them apart with his bare hands.

He is like the friends of Daniel in his generation. Lesser men cower in fear and obey the ungodly demands of the king, but the man who stands for Christ is willing to endure the fiery furnace that rages seven times hotter.

Follow Hard After God

Stirring words about courage and boldness and manhood can inspire a man to believe for a moment that he can conquer the world. But if he is not equipped with a plan to put those words into practice before long, he will retreat into his old self. Our churches and our families do not need any more of those kinds of men. They are useless to the cause of Christ. Our churches and families need men like David, mighty in the Spirit—men after God's own heart.

> *Our churches and families*
> *need men like David,*
> *mighty in the Spirit.*

Many books written for Christian men are often nothing more than a checklist of moral behavior. Read your Bible. . . Go to church. . . Don't look at pornography. . . Yes, all of those are marks of a Christian man, but they do not make a man a Christian. A good and moral man can live his whole life following that kind of checklist and still end up in hell. A Mormon man can be a moral man, but he's not a saved man. A Muslim man can be a moral man, but he needs the Savior. Don't give a man another book of lists to read; give him the Word of God and point him to Christ.

Many men profess Christ because it profits them to do so. Professing to be a Christian may get them a job. Maybe it gets them respect, a position as a deacon or pastor in the church. Maybe they are so good at playing the role of a Christian that they fool many people. If that is you, you are not fooling the Lord Jesus Christ. Let me warn you in love: Ultimately, the only one you are fooling is yourself.

Don't give a man a book of lists to read, give him the Word of God and point him to Christ.

We must not attempt to live good and godly lives in our strength. We must not simply be moral men; we must be mortified men—mortified to this world; mortified to our flesh; men who do all that they do because they are motivated by a genuine love for the Lord Jesus. Love for God must be our greatest motivator. If it is not, whatever else we may do for God will only be wood, hay, and stubble on the day we stand before Him. When those things pass through the fires of testing, they will all burn up.

Love for God must be our greatest motivator.

Sometimes I look around at our generation of men and I can't help but ask myself, Where are the mighty men of God? Where are the men who have counted the cost and stand for Christ? Where are the men whose greatest desire in life is to know and follow hard after God?

This book is one Christian man's attempt to muster the forces. I want to inspire the troops and equip you with practical ideas that have helped me over the years. It won't cover everything (there's so much I'm still learning myself!) but may the Lord use it to awaken those Christian men who may have fallen asleep on the job and to be a refreshing cup of cold water for you who are already faithfully engaged in the thick of the battle. I know the Lord has His remnant in this generation, and I thank God for you!

Let us be men who know and follow hard after God (Psalm 63:8). It is my hope that this small book offers some practical ideas of what that looks like every day.

The Lord Jesus is the Commander of the Armies of Heaven. He is our Captain.

15

When the Bible calls God "The LORD of Hosts" that is military language. The Lord Jesus is the Commander of the Armies of Heaven. He is our Captain. He is leading us. The victory is already won. It was won 2,000 years ago when He died and rose again.

Brother, until the Lord returns we have work to do. And the most important work we have is to lead ourselves and our families in Christian service to the Church and in the world, to the glory of God.

You Must Withstand and Stand

Your Private Life
as a
Christian Man

"What a man is in his prayer
closet is what he is."
(Robert Murray M'Cheyne)

This is where it all starts. At its core, your life is between you and God—no one else. And when you die, you will stand alone before God. As believers, we live in Christian community with one another, but faith in Christ is ultimately an individual matter. Before we can talk about your ministry at home or in the church, we must consider your private life.

(1) Prioritize Prayer and the Scriptures

I have a quotation in a frame that sits next to where I read my Bible every morning. It is a statement by the great Scottish minister, Robert Murray M'Cheyne. It says:

> *What a man is in his prayer closet is what he is.*

Think about that statement. What is a man? We tend to size-up a man many different ways. It may be by what he looks like, or his job, or whether he is rich or poor. But M'Cheyne brings us back to the Word of God. What a man in his in his prayer closet—his private personal life before his Creator—is the true sum of who that man is. This reminds us of what the Lord told Samuel:

> . . . *for man looks at the outward appearance, but the* LORD *looks at the heart.*
> *(1 Samuel 16:7)*

The tragic stories of several men come to mind as I write these words. These men professed to be Christians, yet their private lives were full of sin. These men and their sinful lives grieved their churches and devasted their wives. These are the kind of men Paul wrote to Timothy about. He said that they rejected faith and a good conscience and have had their faith shipwrecked (1 Timothy 1:19).

In that same letter Paul gives a sobering description of such men. He writes, "Some men's sins are clearly evident, preceding them to judgment, but those of some men follow later" (1 Timothy 5:24). Peter also warns that for men like these, "the latter end is worse for them than the beginning," (2 Peter 2:20).

> *Some men's sins are clearly*
> *evident, preceding them to*
> *judgment, but those of some*
> *men follow later*

It is a terrifying thing when a man loses his fear of God. He destroys his life and the lives of everyone around him without any fear of the consequences. He has forgotten that the Bible says, "It is a fearful thing to fall into the hands of the living God" (Hebrews 10:31). May the fear of the Lord cause us to pray the words of David,

> *Search me, O God, and know my heart;*
> *Try me, and know my anxieties;*
> *And see if there is any wicked way in*
> *me,*
> *And lead me in the way everlasting.*
> *(Psalm 139:23-24)*

What does God see when He sees your heart? Who are you in your private life before the Lord? What man are you before God in prayer? That is M'Cheyne's point: Whoever that man is, that is who you are today.

Does that truth alarm you? Does it comfort you? We can all pray more, but are you praying at all? Are you reading the Scriptures daily to know the Lord? My brother likes to put it this way, "We must know the Word of God if we are to know the God of the Word."

We must know the Word of
God if we are to know the
God of the Word.

We must be men of prayer and who read our Bibles daily. And yet, for whatever reasons, many Christian men are not. They rarely pray. They rarely read their Bibles. They may have professed to be Christians for many years, and yet have never read the entire Bible. We need to be men who spend time with the Lord each day in prayer and Bible-reading or we risk becoming like those men with their shipwrecked faith.

May I share an inspiring story with you?

My sister-in-law became a Christian fifty years ago. Over the years she has made it her practice to read through the Bible once a year. The math is easy: She has read the Bible fifty times! What a testimony!

You and I have the greatest privilege a person can have. We can talk with God and hear from Him through His Word. True sheep know the Shepherd. They know His voice and follow Him (John 10:14, 27).

> *We need to be men who*
> *spend time with the Lord*
> *each day in prayer and*
> *Bible-reading. . .*

The importance of prayer cannot be overstated. Isaiah 62:6 speaks of praying so diligently for God to act that those who sought the Lord gave Him no rest.

Jesus highlighted the importance of being persistent in prayer. He told the parable of the man who gave his neighbor no rest in the middle of the night until he finally got up out of bed and gave him bread to feed his guest (Luke 11:5-8).

Jesus also told His disciples a parable

about a widow who sought justice from an unjust judge. She kept coming to him to plead her case and seek justice, so he finally gave in and granted her request. Luke tells his readers why Jesus told that parable, "He spoke a parable to them, *that men always ought to pray and not lose heart. . ."* (Luke 18:1, emphasis added). Isn't that amazing? Over and over in the Scriptures, the Lord invites us to bring our requests to Him, and over and over again He tell us not to give up praying too soon. My brother, keep praying!

We Christian men need to recapture a sense of holy desperation. We need hearts that burn with holy need, with a sense that if we do not have Jesus, we have nothing! Where are the men who cry out to the Lord like Peter did, "Lord, to whom shall we go? You alone have the words of eternal life" (John 6:68).

Don't you think such holy desperation should be in every Christian man's life? After Jesus healed the demon-possessed man, he "begged Him [Jesus] that he might be with Him" (Mark 5:20). If they have truly been saved by Jesus, why do so few Christian men beg to follow Him?

Look at the example of Job. Despite his terrible trials and suffering, despite his moments of doubt, he persisted in following and serving the Lord. The greatest desire of his life was to see God. "How my heart yearns within me!" he said (Job 19:27). Does your heart yearn within you to know and see Jesus?

Does your heart yearn within you to know and see Jesus?

If we are in Christ, then He raised us from death to life. He pulled us out of darkness and brought us into His marvelous light (1 Peter 2:9). He forgave our sins and reconciled us to God (Colossians 3:13; Romans 5:10). We must not let the holy become the commonplace. These are glorious and eternal truths, treasures of God's mercy, love, and grace. We must not lose sight of how precious the Lord Jesus Christ is. We must give Him the preeminence He deserves in our lives. Our hearts should burn with holy desire to follow Him wherever He goes.

(2) Trust God in Trials and Suffering

Amazing Grace is probably the most famous hymn ever written. It tells the story of the wonderful work of God in the life of a believer. It begins at the moment of salvation and ends singing God's praise forever in glory. In the middle of song are the lines,

> *Through many dangers, toils and snares*
> *I have already come,*
> *'Tis grace has brought me safe thus far*
> *And grace will lead me home.*

This verse perfectly describes the Christian life. It is a hard life, filled with "many dangers, toils, and snares [traps]". Besides the ordinary trials of life like flat tires or losing a job, I have known Christians who were robbed at gunpoint. I remember reading about a Christian man and his wife who lost everything they owned when their house burned down. And yet, the Lord promises to use these situations all for our good and His glory (Romans 8:28). The Apostle Paul is a great example of how God uses trials in our lives. As someone pointed out to me not long ago, Paul wrote his most joyful epistle from a Roman jail!

> *There is no school that will make you as wise in the things of God as the school of suffering.*

Of course, our greatest role model of enduring trials and suffering is the Lord Jesus. His whole life was trials and suffering. He was the "Man of sorrows. . .acquainted with grief" (Isaiah 53:3).

Some trials are the ordinary problems of life. Some are long and painful seasons full of sorrow and suffering.

There is no school that will make you as wise in the things of God as the school of suffering. Sometimes we suffer because of someone else's actions. Sometimes we suffer the consequences of our own bad decisions. Sometimes we suffer simply because it is unavoidable in this fallen, suffering world.

It is important to remember that everything that happens in our lives is ordained by God. When the Lord ordains a season of suffering in our lives, He does so in order that we will learn to trust Him more.

Gardiner Spring lived in America in the 1800s and served as the pastor of his church for over sixty years. In his book *The Mission of Sorrow*, he explains how the Lord uses suffering in the life of the Christian to accomplish several purposes. Suffering teaches us submission to God and His will in our lives. It reveals the idols of our hearts and misplaced affections. Though the Lord's hand seems heavy upon us through our suffering, through it we experience the joy of God's comfort and care. When a Christian suffers in this life, it also makes him look forward to heaven where there will be no suffering, only joy forever.

French pastor Adolphe Monod was a man who suffered much in the final years and months of his life. His pulpit ministry was interrupted by sickness several times in his last two years. Weakened by pain and illness, he spent the last five months of his life on his deathbed in agonizing pain and suffering. Despite it all, he said:

I can, by these sufferings, give to God a glory I could not give to Him otherwise. . .[That is why] suffering is a privilege to the Christian, and to suffer much is a special privilege.

Trials and suffering are part of life. Yet, suffering is one of the greatest tools the Lord wisely uses to make us more like Christ and bring glory to Himself.

> *"If you want to be like Jesus, remember, He had a wilderness, a Gethsemane, and a Judas."*

The point of all of this is to reassure you: The Lord can be trusted in trials. As the great revivalist, Leonard Ravenhill, said, "If you want to be like Jesus, remember, He had a wilderness, a Gethsemane, and a Judas."

As a Christian man, how are you enduring your trials? Have you been with the Lord in His school of suffering? If so, you know both the blow of the hammer and yet the tenderness of the Lord's comfort.

How you handle the trials and testing

the Lord sends also influences your wife and family. They will see firsthand how a godly man reacts when the Lord ordains difficult times. My brother, use every trial as an opportunity to grow in Christ and model Christlikeness to your family.

(3) Be Alert Against the Enemy

Spiritual warfare is real; we know that from numerous places in Scripture. But does that mean we are to fear the devil and his forces? Should we worry constantly about the power of their influence in our lives? How do we think of spiritual warfare from a practical, day-to-day, perspective?

Just as some people can err in thinking that spiritual warfare is not real, we can err in thinking Satan is more powerful than he is, or that every negative experience in our life is spiritual warfare. Rather, we should take courage from the fact that the Bible says that God has equipped us for everything we need for the Christian life (2 Peter 1:3), including weapons and strategies for defeating our unseen enemy.

The Lord Jesus taught us to pray,

. . . do not lead us into temptation
But deliver us from the evil one.
(Matthew 6:13)

Jesus would not have taught us to pray this way if there was no such thing as spiritual warfare, or the attacks of a real devil. Instead, He informed us of the danger and taught us our first line of defense against it: to pray to the Father to act on our behalf. And after the ascension of Jesus, the Spirit inspired the writers of the New Testament to give us more guidance.

> *Jesus would not have taught us to pray this way if there was no such thing as spiritual warfare.*

Peter warns us of the danger and tells us to stand fast and resist. "Be sober, be vigilant," he warns, "because your adversary the devil walks about like a roaring lion, seeking whom he may devour. Resist him, steadfast in the faith. . ." (1 Peter 5:8).

Paul also warns his readers of the dangers and gives the tactical guidance needed to "be strong in the Lord and in His mighty power" (Ephesians 6:10). He then describes the Christian's spiritual battle armor, and repeatedly urges believers to be strong, to stand, to pray fervently in the Spirit, to be alert, and to persevere (Ephesians 6:10-18).

James assures us the victory is ours in Christ as he provides the strategy we are to use:

> *Submit to God. Resist the devil and he will flee from you.*
> *(James 4:7)*

John urges us to use our minds, to be discerning, to "test the spirits, whether they are of God" (1 John 4:1).

What I find interesting is that nowhere in Scripture does God say to fear the enemy. We are commanded in many passages to fear the Lord, but never to fear the devil. We are not to take his threats lightly, either, but rather to be aware and on guard against his attacks and prepared for when they come.

For example, in Paul's words about spiritual warfare to the Ephesian believers, he urges them twice to "put on the armor of

God" (11, 13), and four times to withstand or stand (11, 13, 14). He speaks of the Spirit twice (17, 18) and emphasizes the importance of prayer, also mentioned twice (18).

Space prevents us from looking at this topic in more detail, but it is worth pointing out from the above passages how proactive we are to be in battle.

We are commanded in many
passages to fear the Lord,
but never to fear the devil.

The Lord has equipped us with all the spiritual resources and strategies we will ever need to stand boldly against the enemy's attacks, and they are "mighty in God for pulling down strongholds" (2 Corinthians 10:4).

Most wonderfully of all, the Lord Jesus Himself prayed for His disciples, asking the Father to, "keep them from the evil one" (John 17:15). Jesus was interceding for all believers, all whom the Father gave Him. What a comfort!

So, what does all of this look like in day-today living? Our primary focus is to be on the Lord. When we focus on Him, seeking after Him in prayer and the Word and doing those good works that please Him, it becomes much easier to fight against our own sin. For myself, I rarely tend to think of spiritual warfare at all. I'm sure I do, but it is in the back of my mind. I am not minimizing the power and temptations of the devil when I say this, but most days I am more concerned about the weaknesses and sin in my own heart than of the devil and his minions around me.

Yes, be mindful of spiritual warfare. Yes, be on guard against what tempts you specifically, and at what times those temptations come. But there is no need to dwell on those things or live in fear. Pray to the Father. Follow Christ. Walk in the Spirit.

(4) Always Be Ready

There is one more important point I want to encourage you about in your personal walk with Christ. You may be wondering, How can I know if my private life is in order?

First, understand that having our private

lives in order is not a one-time event. It is true, of course, that when we are born again, we become a new creation and the old is passed away (2 Corinthians 5:17). At the time we repent and believe the gospel, through Christ and the power of the Spirit our old sinful hearts of stone are replaced with new hearts of flesh, made pure by faith (Ezekiel 36:26; Acts 15:9).

> *When we are born again, we become a new creation and the old is passed away.*

However, as Christians we still sin. James, for example, warns believers about having "bitter envy and self-seeking" in their hearts (James 3:14). In his prayer of repentance David asked the Lord to create a clean heart in him and restore a right spirit (Psalm 51:10). When we sin we also need to go to the Lord and seek His forgiveness (1 John 1:9).

The first practical way to keep our private lives in order is to walk with the Lord each day. Jesus told us to abide in Him, and that without Him we can do nothing (John 15:5). As we draw close to the Lord in prayer and read the Bible each day, the Lord will give us assurance that all is well, or He will lovingly send the Spirit to show us what we need to know, change, or confess.

Some years ago, I heard wise advice I have never forgotten, "A pastor ought to be ready at any moment to pray, preach, or die." Those are wise words, and I would say they are not for pastors only. I'm not a pastor but ever since I heard those words, I have tried to live my life by them.

> *You ought to be ready*
> *at any moment to pray,*
> *preach, or die.*

Paul directed Timothy to be always ready to preach the gospel (2 Timothy 4:2). In his first epistle, Peter tells his readers that since the end is near, they ought to be clear-headed so they can pray (1 Peter 4:7).

On a related note, I have also heard it said that at any given time, a Christian is coming out of a trial, heading into one, or already in the middle of a trial. It would be wise if we would also live our lives so we are thankful the Lord has us in a place of calm and blessing, but not to get too comfortable there. Jonah enjoyed the shade of his melon plant, but it didn't last very long. No need to live in dread and anticipation, but it's wise to always be ready for trials.

The message the Lord gave the prophet Haggai to take to the people of Judah was, "Consider your ways!" It was a call to examine themselves and their faithfulness before the Lord. We all need to do that from time to time. Before moving on to the next chapter, ask the Holy Spirit to show you your heart. Ask the Lord to remove anything that needs to be removed and to purify whatever needs to be made pure.

How can we men love and serve our wives and families well if our private lives are a mess? How can we be faithful churchmen and ministers of Christ, whether we are pastors or not, if are not daily walking in the Spirit? We can't. Like Jesus said, without Him we can do nothing.

Ask yourself:

- Is my heart right to pray to the Lord without hinderance?
- Am I spiritually prepared to preach or evangelize at a moment's notice?

- If the Lord were to take me home today, am I ready?

The writer of Hebrews reminds us that our consciences are cleansed by the blood of Jesus for a purpose: so that we can serve God (Hebrews 9:14). Paul expresses this same idea in his letter to the Ephesians. He tells his readers they have been made alive in Christ and have been created to do good works in Christ (Ephesians 2:10).

This world desperately needs to see men living their lives for Christ, full of love and good works.

Our wives deserve godly husbands. Our families deserve godly fathers. Our churches need godly churchmen. And this world desperately needs to see men living their lives for Christ, full of love and good works, to the glory of God.

We have no time to waste!

Your Private Life as a Christian Man

Your Marriage and Your Home

"Husbands, likewise, dwell with [your wives] with understanding, giving honor to the wife, as to the weaker vessel, and as being heirs together of the grace of life, that your prayers may not be hindered."
(1 Peter 3:7)

Having talked about a man's private life, it is time to talk about his marriage and his home. Although they are discussed together in this chapter, marriage and home are not equal. A man's marriage takes priority over the family dynamics of the children (who, in turn, take priority over a man's extended family).

> *A man's marriage takes*
> *priority over the family*
> *dynamics of the children. . .*

Your God-given roles as a husband and as a father are the two most important roles you will have in your life. No other roles will impact generations like how you love your wife and model Christ in your home. As you do so, you also show a lost and dying world God's wise plan for the family and the home, to the praise of His Name.

(1) Know the Sanctifying Power of Your Home

It has been my experience that a man's greatest measure of sanctification—that is, being set apart from sin and set apart to serve God—will take place in the home. I can't think of any environment that has made me who I am today as much as endeavoring to be a godly husband, even more than seminary, work, or ministry. And although I am not a father, I am sure those of you who are would agree.

That brings up an important point about families I heard years ago that I want to pass along to you: Your wife is your family. When children come along, your family grows, but for now, if it is just you and your wife, you are a *family*.

First, marriage itself is sanctifying. In a sermon I heard years ago called, "The Glory of God in Marriage," Paul Washer talks about how God does not pair you up with someone who is just like you. Rather, your mate will likely be very different than you. The Lord does this in wisdom, so that by learning to live with your differences, you are taught patience, kindness, grace, and all the qualities God desires in your life.

The Lord also uses the ordinary pressures and problems of home life for His purposes. Of course, God is infinite, so He has an infinite number of ways at His disposal to accomplish this. Sometimes they are the moment-by-moment ordinary details of life; at other times they are specific seasons or trials He allows. Every time the roof leaks or a child is sick or there is a problem at work, this is an opportunity to learn how to trust the Lord, obey His commands, and glorify Him.

Sanctification is being set apart from sin and set apart to serve God.

Home is where the Lord teaches us virtues like humility and forgiveness. Being a husband and father can be very humbling at times, especially when we sin with our words or actions and need to humble ourselves and ask forgiveness from our wife or children. It's also where we learn to forgive others when they sin against us.

Home is the main place the Lord teaches us to be patient. Jacob knew he had to lead his family procession slowly, so as not to push the children, and livestock too hard (Genesis 33:14,15). We need to be lovingly aware of our family's limits and patient when life doesn't move at the pace we want.

Patience also comes in the form of interruptions. Consider the earthly ministry of our Lord. As you read the Gospels, His ministry seems like one interruption after another. In Matthew 9 alone first we see a ruler come to Him asking Him to heal his daughter (verse 9). On the way, a woman reaches out to be healed (verse 20). After He raises the young girl from the dead, two blind men follow and interrupt Him (verse 27). Then a mute man is brought to Him to be healed (verse 32). Matthew then explains to his readers that these kinds of things happened everywhere Jesus went (verse 35). But the Lord was always willing, never rushed, never too busy to show compassion (verse 36).

We need to be lovingly aware of our family's limits.

Who is more helpless and in need of tender loving care than a baby? Who needs nurture and encouragement more than a child? Who deserves our loving partnership more than our wife? Home is where we are constantly learning kindness and compassion, and to practice love and good works.

- HOME is where we learn to communicate. God uses our families to teach us how to listen, how to have empathy, what to say, and how best to say it.
- HOME is also where the Lord trains us to seek Him for wisdom and to apply biblical principles to solve our problems.
- HOME is where we discover just how much our attitude affects our wife and children. In fact, this lesson has been so important in my life that I have dedicated a whole topic on it that we will get to soon.

God continues to work these virtues into my life. In the process of leading in my home, God has taught me leadership. At home, at work and in ministry, I am a better leader because the Lord has taught me to be a better servant.

As we conclude this section, let us remember that every word and action of the Lord Jesus is a lesson for us to apply in our lives and in our homes. Look how tender He was to children! Look how compassionate He was to women! Look how He taught His disciples! Think about just His final day on earth. The Lord arranged the place for the Passover meal for His disciples, washed their feet, taught them, prayed to the Father for them, protected them at His arrest, and cared about Peter during His own trial. And as He hung in His agony there on the cross, He made sure His mother would be cared for. Oh, that we would look to Jesus as our example of how to love and serve our family with patience, grace, and compassion!

(2) Practice Love and Good Works at Home

When Jesus was asked which was the greatest commandment, He replied, "'You shall love the Lord your God with all your heart, with all your soul, and with all your mind.' This is the first and great commandment. And the second is like it: 'You shall love your neighbor as yourself,'" (Matthew 22:37-39).

Here we must ask ourselves: Who is our neighbor? Our neighbor is anyone around us. So, it makes sense, then, that our closest neighbors are the ones nearest to us, our wife and children. They are our "neighbors" who happen to live under the same roof we do.

Home is our closest mission field, the place where we can sow love and good works and reap a harvest for many years to come. It is where we preach to our wife and little ones that Christ is crucified, risen, and returning. And it is the first place we are to stoop down and serve in humility with the basin and the towel.

God has wisely divided up
the roles within the home.

Yet, for some Christian men home is not a place to serve but to be served. Home becomes the place they can hang up their

Christianity for the day and pick it up again tomorrow as they head out the door.

God has wisely divided up the roles within the home. The wife is to care for her husband, their children, and the home, and the man is to work provide for all of them, lead them in love, and be the spiritual head of the home. But we husbands can serve our wives by helping around the house, for example.

When Paul wrote to Titus, he told him, "Those who have believed in God should be careful to maintain good works. These things are good and profitable to men" (Titus 3:8). Where should good works start if not at home?

The Lord Jesus was a burden-lifter. He lifted burdens from others and bore them on His own shoulders (Isaiah 53:4). He took burdens off the sick, the demon-possessed, the mourners, the shamed outcast. . .And most of all, He took upon Himself the burden of the sins of the world. The Lord graciously says over and over that we are to give Him our burdens (Psalm 55:22; Matthew 11:28; 1 Peter 5:7).

Since we men are to love our wives as

Christ loved the church, we ought to be sensitive to the burdens of our loved ones. What burdens can you lift off your wife today? What burdens from off the backs of your dear children? How can you glorify the Lord in your good works at home?

Let me add one final thought here, not so much about good works but about good *words*. Just as you aim to model love and good works at home, model Jesus in how you and your wife speak about each other in public.

> *The Lord Jesus was a burden-lifter. He lifted burdens from others and bore them on His own shoulders.*

Another wise word I heard years ago is: Husbands and wives should agree not to correct or criticize the other in public. Model being a loving, Christlike husband by always speaking well of your wife when speaking to others. Think how good your wife will feel when she hears you speaking well of her to others. Think how good you will feel when she speaks kind words about you, too. She will be modeling being a godly wife who honors her husband when she chooses to not correct or criticize you publicly. Instead of using your words to tear down, together you will be serving the Lord in a public ministry of grace, building up one another in love.

(3) Model Christ in Your Home

This section overlaps and continues the discussion of love and good works at home. It's about how our family watches us and what we can teach them by how we act and react in daily life. Our wives will learn more from us by observing our lives than by anything we could say. Actions really do speak louder than words.

Let me share a quick example. I know a Christian man whose wife did not always read the Bible. She read many Christian books, but never developed a pattern of regular time in the Word.

He, on the other hand, had made it a priority to start every morning with a time of reading his Bible.

His wife's lack of Bible reading bothered him. At times he tried to criticize her lack of Bible reading, but that did not work. Meanwhile, every morning, he kept to his pattern of reading the Bible.

Over time, his wife began to read her Bible more regularly. Eventually she, too, made it her daily habit to start her day reading a passage of Scripture!

What changed?

She began to notice the effect daily Bible reading had on his life. He was growing in the Lord in ways she was not. So, she decided to start reading the Bible for herself.

All the while, he had no idea of the effect of his witness. He had no idea she was watching his life, or the inspiration he had become!

Whether it is our habit of daily Bible reading and prayer, how we handle the daily pressures of life, or sudden trials, our wives will learn more from us by observing us daily and in trials than they ever will by our sermons (or our nagging—and yes, we men can be nags too!). What do they see in you when you face trials? Discouragements? Disappointments?

Look at how Peter describes Jesus in Acts 10:38: "God anointed Jesus of Nazareth with the Holy Spirit and with power, *who went about doing good and healing* all who were oppressed by the devil," (emphasis added). Did you know that the word "Christian" really means "one who is of Christ"? Early believers were so like Jesus in how they lived that they were given this nickname. How can you follow the blessed example of Jesus and be like Him? Why not make it a point every day to go around doing good wherever you go, and when you have the chance, share the healing words of the good news about Jesus to a world that is oppressed by the devil.

And where does that start? Right under your roof, in your own home. Ask the Lord to make you like Jesus today.

How do you model Christ to your wife? Do you love her as Christ loved the church? Do you prize her as the weaker (more delicate) vessel? Do you encourage her with kind words? Is she comforted by your words? Does she know that you will protect and care for her? Does she see you reading your Bible? Does she think of you as a man of earnest prayer?

*Our wives will learn more
from us by observing us
daily and in trials than they
ever will by our sermons.*

Your wife is a gift from God. God has uniquely gifted her to complement you. When I am stuck on a decision and I need another opinion, I will talk it over with my wife. She has a wonderful way of pointing out a detail I had not considered. Very often that detail was the part that jammed up the whole works and once removed, the decision is obvious and there is a good way forward.

Do you value your wife's input on important decisions? Does she know that you do?

Do you express appreciation for how she keeps the home, the meals she prepares, and how she raises the children?

Because I don't have children myself, I can only talk it about being a father in general terms. But I will tell you about my own father.

I grew up with a loving father. I never saw him drunk. He never beat us or my mother. He was a faithful husband to my mother, and he made many sacrifices to provide for us children.

He was a good man, but he was not a Christian man. He rarely went to church. He did not lead us in the things of the Lord. I think I saw him reading a Bible one time in my life, but I never saw him in earnest prayer.

Because of this, I did not grow up with the blessing of learning how to be a godly Christian man by watching my father's life. I never experienced those moments of a wise, godly father teaching his son what he needs to know about life from God's Word.

Will your children have memories of walking into the room and seeing you, their father, reading his Bible or praying? What impressions will you leave with them? What will they tell *their* grandchildren—your great-grandchildren—about you? Imagine the power of your testimony so that even your fourth generation from now could know that Christ was the Lord of your life!

(4) Lead with a Christlike Attitude

The previous section focused on how we act and react at home. This section talks about having a Christlike attitude at home.

Our attitude at home matters more than we think. You set the temperature in your home. Because of you, your home will either be like a warm fire or a cold wind. The entire family feels hot or cold based on your temperament.

If the sun in your life is hidden behind clouds, your family will feel the chill in the air. When you are angry and inside you are full of thunder and storms, your anger will cause them to seek cover. Your dark clouds of despair will cause them to be sad or afraid.

But the opposite is also true. When your steadfast hope and trust in the Lord shines bright, the whole family will want to come out and enjoy its warmth. When you show them what calm assurance in the Lord's providence looks like when you face uncertainty or trials, your attitude will inspire, calm, and cheer them. They will know that that the storm will pass, and until it does, you all are safe, just like Noah was in the ark—and remember, the ark is a kind of picture of Christ.

We need to be men who demonstrate strong confidence in the goodness of God. We need to lead our families the way Joshua did, with that same resolve he showed when he said, "But as for me and my house, we will serve the Lord," (Joshua 24:15).

How can we do this? In the world, emotions often rule. I have heard it explained this way: Emotions are the locomotive at the front of the train. But that's now how it works for the Christian. In Christ our minds have been renewed. Our wills have been renewed. We are no longer held back and enslaved by our passions.

As they teach in Biblical counseling, right thoughts lead to right actions, lead to right feelings. When we think right, we do right; and when we do right, we feel right.

Our mind becomes the locomotive, which lead our actions, with our emotions connected at the end of the train.

That is why as Christians we can enjoy peace that passes understanding (Philippians 4:7). We are not letting our situation determine our emotions, but rather are reminding ourselves of who God is, and His great and precious promises.

*We need to be men
who demonstrate strong
confidence in the goodness
of God. We need to serve
our families with a spirit
of cheerfulness.*

We need to serve our families with a spirit of cheerfulness. Think of Paul's words to the Galatians, "The fruit of the Spirit is love, joy, peace, longsuffering, kindness, goodness, faithfulness, gentleness, self-control," (Galatians 5:22-23). How can you model those virtues to your family?

Look again at the example of our Lord. Though He was the Man of Sorrows, He was full of joy and cheerfulness. Again and again He is recorded as saying to someone, "Be of good cheer!" To the paralytic whose sins were forgiven He said, "Be of good cheer!" To the woman healed from her years suffering from her blood disease He said, "Be of good cheer!" All four Gospels record Him saying it. Even though He said trials were sure to come, He told His disciples to "Be of good cheer!" Why? "I have overcome the world" (John 16:33).

Think about how one look from Him must have inspired joy and a cheerful heart! Think of the encouragement the forgiven thief on the cross must have had after being told he would soon be with the Lord in paradise!

> *Jesus told His disciples to*
> *"Be of good cheer!" Why?*
> *"I have overcome the world."*

In this world it is easy to lose sight of our reasons to be cheerful. It is easy to come home tired and discouraged from counseling a hardened heart or hearing an unjust criticism. To be in ministry is to deal with the heartaches of sin up close and personal. It can be sad, heavy work.

But don't let the devil steal your joy. Don't let your flesh and your emotions determine your attitude. Think about the spirit you are about to bring home to your beautiful wife and children. Think of the blessings they are from the Lord. Then look to the Lord Jesus and "Be of good cheer!"

Your Ministry

"Meditate on these things; give yourself entirely to them, that your progress may be evident to all. Take heed to yourself and to the doctrine. Continue in them, for in doing this you will save both yourself and those who hear you."
(1 Timothy 4:15-16)

Many men wrestle with ministry burn-out. Over time, church life demands more and more of their time and energy. Because they do not know how to say no, they get overcommitted with appointments and responsibilities. When this happens, a man's wife and marriage are the first to feel the effects. Then the children. Left uncorrected, his home life becomes a quiet disaster. Like a car that is not properly maintained, a man can run for while like this, but, like the car, eventually he is going to break down.

The Lord did not intend for ministry to be like that. This final chapter offers practical help for balancing your family and your ministry.

(1) Practice Loving Discretion

Years ago when I thought the Lord was leading me to be a pastor, I informed my wife
that there would be some details in ministry
I would not tell her. I did not make a list of
what I would and would not share, and it was
not that I would plan to keep secrets because
I did not love and trust her. Rather, I would
not tell her everything precisely *because* I
loved her.

My reasoning was that I would not want to
share sensitive details about certain people
or difficult circumstances because I did not
want to burden her. I'm not talking about
regular conversations about church life. I
mean those difficult problems that arise in
ministry. I was practicing loving discretion.

What if I told her something about
someone and then she was never able to
look at that person the same again? What if
knowing became a stumbling block to her
being able to love that person in the Lord?
Also, no one could accuse her meddling in
church leadership matters if she had no idea
what they were!

There is no Bible verse that says, "Do not

tell your wife about ministry details." Maybe some men are different, and they tell their wife everything about ministry life. There is no rule here; this is only my suggestion for you to do with as you like.

Also, loving discretion happens on a case-by-case basis. There have been times I have told my wife details about a particular church situation because she needed to know. She needed to know so she could pray more specifically about it. Or she needed to know because I wanted her to meet with a sister in Christ to try to disciple her as she was going through some trial, or for some other reason.

And the opposite is true: I have asked my wife not to tell me details about the women she counsels and disciples unless she decides otherwise. Most of the time I have either no idea what is going, or just a general idea of the situation. For one thing, I'm not the pastor, so if it is really a serious matter, she can ask the elders for advice. Also, as a man I don't need to know certain details.

On a related note, years ago someone gave me another great piece of advice that I have always sought to live by. That person said,

"Be a deep well." When you drop a stone into a well it goes down, down, down, never to come up again.

When someone tells you something in confidence, let it sink to the bottom. Don't bring it up to others. Obviously, this also is not a firm rule and requires sound judgment. There are times when others need to be made aware of a matter. But, in general people should be able to trust you with a confidential matter.

(2) Don't Neglect your Family for Ministry

Speaking about the family, my pastor, Dr. J. Paul Dean, once said:

> In God's created order, the family is foundational. . . .If Satan wants to destroy a culture, he attacks the family.

He is right. And related to that, when Satan wants to destroy a man of God, he will attack him personally and attack his family. And yet, many pastors and churchmen prioritize their ministries over their families.

*Don't sacrifice your wife and
family for ministry.*

To put it plainly: Don't sacrifice your wife and family for ministry. Biblical counselor Dr. Jay E. Adams writes of the need for balance when it comes to juggling church and family. He begins by saying that if we neglect our families for the work of the church, we are in sin, and the local church is also in sin for letting it happen. Then Dr. Adams adds:

> *A minister, for instance, who "sacrifices" his family for the "work [of the ministry]" is wrong. He has an unbiblical attitude toward his family. He is to be a husband to his wife as Christ is to the church; a father to his children as God is a Father to us. Does Christ "sacrifice" His church for the sake of His work? Does God do so with His children? There is no such concept taught in the Bible.[1]*

---

1 Jay E. Adams, *Maintaining the Delicate Balance in Christian Living*, (Timeless Texts, Woodruff, South Carolina)105.

Some people may say that the demands of ministry are so great that they require such neglect, but that is simply not true. Despite often working eighteen hours a day preaching, teaching, or writing, Charles Spurgeon was a loving, joyful father.

Dr. Martyn Lloyd-Jones, like Spurgeon before him, also kept a remarkably busy ministry schedule. Yet, Lloyd-Jones did not sacrifice his family for greater ministry either. He also is remembered as a loving and devoted husband, father, and grandfather.

Some people may say that the demands of ministry are so great that they require such neglect, but that is simply not true.

By contrast, the great A.W. Tozer was also used mightily by God but his family legacy is quite different. Tozer's home life was bleak. Although Tozer loved children, he was cold and distant to his wife and his own children. Is that kind of ministry legacy worth it? It's better to have no success in ministry at all than great success at the expense of your family.

Your wife is your first priority in ministry. She is not your only ministry, but she is your *first* ministry. Your children are second—which also means they are not on par with your wife. Then comes everything else. How and what this looks like is something for you to consider as an individual matter. It may depend on the personalities of you and your wife, what stage of life you are both in, the ages and life stages of your children, the particular circumstances at church, etc.

As in all areas of life, love is to be your guide. What does loving your wife and family look like at this stage? Is your conscience clear before the Lord that you are doing your best to love your wife as Christ loved the church? Are you making time to love and model Christ to your children? Also, Scripture says they are a gift from the Lord. Are you taking time to enjoy and delight in these precious gifts He has given you? These years will speed by; don't miss them.

(3) Take Control of Your Time and Your Commitments

John Calvin famously said, "The heart is an idol factory." Our hearts are constantly making new idols that distract us and entice us away from the Lord. Those idols can be pleasures, but we can also make an idol out of work. Jesus told the parable of the rich man and his barn as a warning against storing up treasures on earth—but how did the man get so rich? It could be that he never stopped working. Work and material gain were the idols he worshiped in his heart.

> *John Calvin famously said,*
> *"The heart is an*
> *idol factory."*

A businessman can make an idol out of his career. If he is successful in business, there is always the temptation to work harder to be even more successful. He may take a job that keeps him away from his wife and children for long periods because the money seems too good to resist. Over time, he becomes the kind of man our Lord spoke about when He asked, "For what will it profit a man if he gains the whole world, and loses his own soul?" (Mark 8:36).

There is also a risk of being too busy with church and ministry life. The demands on the married seminary student may cause him to spend more time with his books than his own family. The pressures of ministry can overwhelm a man little by little, just like when someone is dragged out to sea with the tide.

Here again, there is no set rule of what that looks like, but if you are running ragged with appointments and obligations, that should serve as a warning there is a problem.

I want to offer three practical ways to help guard against over commitment.

FIRST, talk with your wife. The Lord has given her to you as your helpmate. She is the one who knows you better than anyone else. Ask her if she thinks your ministry schedule is becoming dangerously close to unhealthy, or even sinful. Does she think you have to attend too many meetings? When you are home, does she feel she and the children really have your attention, or are you distracted by all that you have going on? There are certainly seasons where ministry demands are higher than usual, but those should be exceptions, and this should not be the normal routine of life.

A SECOND PRACTICAL WAY to avoid over-commitment in ministry is simply to learn to say no. Not every opportunity is of the Lord. And some opportunities may be the Lord's way of testing your resolve; will you be able to set boundaries and say no? Be discerning. Use wisdom. Say no when appropriate. If you chose wrongly, the Lord will bring the opportunity around again.

LASTLY, a final way to guard against over-commitment is to reserve time for your wife and family. In time-oriented cultures, whatever holds the reins of the calendar directs the rest of life. There is no need to explain to someone why you can't make a meeting. Just tell them, "I already have an appointment." You do: Your family. Be sure to block out time for just you and your wife, as well as times for your wife and children. Be king of your calendar.

(4) Get Wisdom for Life-Changing Decisions

If we are to lead ourselves, our marriage, our family, and our ministry well, we need wisdom. So, what exactly is wisdom? Wisdom is simply this: Applying God's Word to everyday life.

> *Wisdom is simply applying God's Word to everyday life.*

The Scriptures are our guide for a life that pleases the Lord. That's why the Bible says that the fear of the Lord is beginning of wisdom (Proverbs 1:7). I once heard Dr. Stuart Scott explain it this way:

> *The knowledge of God leads to the fear of God, which leads to loving God, which leads to loving others.*

We must know the Lord if we are to have wisdom, love God, and love others.

To get wisdom, we must be regularly spending time in God's Word. Then, as situations come up in everyday life, we can think back to what we read. We ask ourselves, What does Scripture say about my situation? What principles apply to my problem? What examples can I think of from Scripture that may apply to my circumstances?

Suppose you are offered a job. You have a decision to make. Do you say yes and take the job, or not? Just because the opportunity presented itself does not mean it is from the Lord. Before you can decide, you need to ask questions and consider the offer from all angles. Gather as much data as you can, then the Lord will make the decision clear.

*What does Scripture say
about my situation?*

For example, I was once offered a job with a ministry in another state. I accepted the position before understanding all that would be involved. In God's mercy, I quickly calculated that the cost of moving and the expenses in the new city would be too much of a burden on our family. There is a lot more to the story, but at the same time the Lord also presented an opportunity that would not require such upheaval. I quickly backed out of the opportunity out of state and accepted the one that would not upset our home life. I learned the lesson: Do not pull up roots or make a life-changing decision (new church, moving, etc.,) without doing your research and considering how it may impact your marriage and family.

> *I learned the lesson: Do not pull up roots or make a life-changing decision without doing your research!*

In discussing how the Lord leads us in life, a dear brother in the Lord has often quoted the words of Abraham's servant to me. In Genesis 24 we read how Abraham sent his servant in search of a wife for his son Isaac. Through a remarkable series of events the servant could not have possibly arranged on his own, the Lord led him to Rebekah. When asked how it all happened, the servant testified to God's careful leading. He said, "As for me, being on the way, the Lord led me. . ." (Genesis 24:27).

We can't always apply a specific chapter and verse to life. There are no Bible verses that tell us what job to take, where to live, or who to marry. But by looking at principles in God's Word, we can gain wisdom to make wise decisions.

We can also get wisdom by observing life. Solomon did this a lot. Many of his proverbs were written because he was inspired by what he noticed in nature and in life. In Chapter 24 of Proverbs, he talks about what he learned walking by the overgrown field of a lazy man and walking past a vineyard of a foolish man who didn't fix its broken-down walls. He says, "When I saw it, I considered it. . .I looked on it and received instruction," (Proverbs 24:32).

Proverbs 24:3-4 says, "Through wisdom a house is built. . .By knowledge the rooms are filled with all precious and pleasant riches." Whether you are a pastor, deacon, or faithful church member, determine to build the "house" of your ministry (and your life) with wisdom. Over the years, furnish it with the "precious and pleasant riches" of God's Word.

A Final Word of Encouragement to You

". . .let us run with endurance the
race that is set before us, looking
unto Jesus, the author and
finisher of our faith. . ."
(Hebrews 12:1-2)

A few years ago, I read the journals of the great evangelist, George Whitefield. What impressed me most was not the crowds he preached to. It was not the way the Lord used him, although that did make an impression on me. What most impressed me was that Whitefield was constantly viewing all of life through the lens of Scripture. In every experience he had, great or small, he thought of a portion of Scripture that he felt applied to the situation. Like the apostle Paul, Whitefield took Christ as his comfort and encouragement "everywhere and in all things," (Philippians 4:12). Whitefield was content in Christ.

My hope is that this little book has refreshed your spirit and pointed you to the comforts and strength we have in our Lord Jesus Christ. Though in our world we are often troubled by temptations, trials, and suffering, Christ is our soul's anchor

(Hebrews 6:19). Whatever uncertainties of life you may face, whatever sorrows over the years of your ministry, the Lord is righteous in your midst, and He never fails (Zephaniah 3:5).

I long for the day we are clothed in white robes, holding palm branches, and singing, "Salvation belongs to our God who sits on the throne, and to the Lamb!" (Revelation 7:10). Until then, may the Lord bless you, your wife, your family, and all your labors for Him.

A Final Word of Encouragement to You

A Word to Your Godly Wife

"Who can find a virtuous wife?
For her worth is far
above rubies."
(Proverbs 31:10)

Although this is a book for Christian men, much of the material can be applied to wives in their respective roles and ministries. The role of a wife in Christian service cannot be overstated. Any man blessed to have a woman like Priscilla laboring with him for Christ is blessed indeed! I am certainly thankful for my "Priscilla," my wife Amy. Amy faithfully serves in prayer ministries, in counseling and discipleship, encouragement, and much, much more.

That's why I asked her to offer her suggestions for other ladies. In the following few pages, she shares her list of some of the important ministry lessons she thought to share with ministry wives. These are not listed in any particular order.

Important Ministry Lessons

- It is essential for a wife to pray regularly for her husband's eyes and heart to be guarded from temptation. Men are tempted in ways we are not.
- Practice loving discretion about what you share with your husband about the women you disciple and counsel.
- Similarly, be careful whom you share with, and how much you share, with regard to other members of the church.
- Be willing to listen and ask questions of your husband. Do not be overbearing, but offer a supportive, listening ear.
- Also, be willing *not* to ask questions. Sometimes it requires prayerful wisdom to wait and allow him to direct the conversation.
- A pastor's wife doesn't need to know everything, and sometimes it's best she doesn't.
- Remember God's order: a woman's

focus is on the Lord first and foremost, then her husband, then her children. Don't make your children into idols.

- Pray for your husband in *all* things.
- While you may pray for the Lord to change your husband's heart in a matter, be sure to also pray that the Lord shows you the ways your heart may need to change.
- Seek to have a humble spirit. Be open to teaching and to loving correction.
- Make time to read your Bible every day. You cannot speak the gospel to yourself, teach your children, or be a helper to your husband if you are not in the Word daily.
- Cling to the Lord. Your identity is in Christ and not who other people think you should be or how they think you should act.
- Focus on being Christlike and acting biblically. Do not feel obligated to conform to the congregation's perception of what a pastor's wife should be, or how she should act.

Honor the Lord and your husband, and the Lord will take care of the rest.

- Trust the Lord in all things
. . .Even though you do not under-stand;
. . .Even though the timing seems wrong (not fast enough for you, not the "right" time, etc.);
. . .Even though the world tells you differently.

- Do the next thing. On the hard days, in the midst of trials, trust the Lord and do the next thing, no matter how small. Then do the next thing after that. . .

- Remember: God hears and sees what is in your heart. Being obedient to the Lord includes what goes on in our minds and hearts, as well as the words we speak.

- Be guided by Proverbs 3:5-6.

A Word to Your Godly Wife

Study Guide

You Must
Withstand and Stand

- What are some trends and influences you believe you need to "withstand" in the culture today?
- What are some ways God has called you to be a leader?
- Read 2 Peter 2:4-8. What challenges did Noah and Lot face?
- What are some challenges you face in your role as a leader at home and in the ministry area God has called you?
- Why must love for God be our greatest motivator? (p14). What happens if we attempt to live for Christ in our own strength?
- How can thinking about Christ's victory apply and inspire you in your everyday life?

Your Private Life as a Christian Man
· · · · · · · · · · · · · · · · · · · ·

(1) Prioritize Prayer and the Scriptures

- What do you think about Robert Murray M'Cheyne's statement *What a man is in his prayer closet is what he is*?
- Have you ever known a man who professed Christ and later walked away from the faith?
- What do you think about the statement *We must know the Word of God if we are to know the God of the Word*?
- What is your typical routine for time with the Lord (prayer and Bible reading)? Do you have a set time?
- We can all improve our times with the Lord. What action can you take this week to know and love the Lord more?
- Page 25 discusses several life-changing truths about what Jesus did for us and to us. What

should our response be to Him for
all He has done for us?

(2) Trust God in Trials
and Suffering

- What encouragement of God's
  faithfulness would you share with
  a Christian brother going through
  trials?
- Paul wrote his most joyful epistle
  (Philippians) from a Roman prison
  cell. What does that say about God's
  faithfulness to us in our trials?
- Jesus' whole life involved trials and
  suffering. What examples of these
  can you think of?
- How does thinking about Jesus and
  how He endured His trials affect
  your thoughts of Him?
- What do you think Pastor Monod
  meant when he said, "Suffering is a
  privilege to the Christian"?
- Have you ever known a Christian or
  Christians who had to endure great
  trials and suffering? How would you

describe their relationship with the Lord? What were they like? Were they joyful? Bitter?

(3) Be Alert Against the Enemy

- Read 1 Peter 5:8. Why do you suppose Peter wrote that to his first readers? From the text, are we helpless to resist the devil? Why or why not?
- What do Ephesians 6:10, 1 Peter 5:8, and James 4:7 all have in common? (*Hint: What is the source of our strength?*)
- What are some resources and strategies the Lord has equipped us with for spiritual warfare?
- How can focusing on the Lord (instead of the devil) be a strategy in spiritual warfare?
- Thinking back over everything you have read so far, what are some practical ways you can focus on the Lord?
- What are some ways to be on guard against temptations?

(4) Always Be Ready

- This chapter begins with the statement, "Having our private lives in order is not a one-time event." What does that mean? Do you agree or disagree?
- How does a daily walk with God result in a well-ordered private life?
- Read 1 Peter 4:7. What does this verse suggest about Peter's view of the importance of prayer in our lives?
- Read John 15:5. How can you apply that truth your everyday life?
- Have you ever been asked at a moment's notice to pray or give your testimony or share a devotional thought in a group? What happened?
- Read Hebrews 9:14. What are "dead works"? What are some ways "to serve the living God"?

Your Marriage and Your Home
· · · · · · · · · · · · · · · · · · · ·

(1) Know the Sanctifying Power of Your Home

- What are some ways your home life has helped you grow as a Christian?
- If you are married, what are some ways you and your wife are different? How has God used those differences to help mature you in Christ?
- What are some areas God has designed your wife to complement you? What are some areas she is naturally gifted in that you are lacking, and vice versa?
- How can you practice humility, forgiveness, and patience in your home?
- What ways can you look to Jesus as your example to be a faithful husband and father in your home?
- What is one virtue you would most like the Lord to work into your life over the next six months? Do you

think you need to be more loving? Patient? Humble? Forgiving? What can you do to increase that virtue in your heart?

(2) Practice Love and Good Works at Home

- What does loving your neighbor look like when your "neighbor" is your wife and children?
- What are some ways your home is your closest mission field?
- Practicing love and good works are not just actions. They begin as an attitude of the heart. What are some ideas for practicing love and good works at home?
- How has Jesus been a burden-lifter in your life?
- How can you model Christ and be a burden-lifter to your wife and children?
- Have you ever noticed if you and your wife correct or criticize each other publicly? Discuss the idea of

agreeing to not correct/criticize in public with your wife. What does she think about it?

(3) Model Christ in Your Home

- Have you ever noticed that your life and conduct are observed even in your own home? If so, what effect has this had on you, if any?
- Read Acts 10:38. Consider Peter's description of Jesus' life and ministry. What are some ways we can seek to be like Jesus in our spheres of influence?
- What are some ways your father influenced you as you were growing up? If you did not have your father, maybe say something about an uncle, grandfather, or other father figure who meant a lot to you. What did you learn from him?
- What would you like your children to say about you after you are gone?
- What impression would you like to leave in the minds and hearts of your grandchildren?

(4) Lead with a Christlike Attitude

- This chapter discusses how our attitudes "set the temperature" of the home. Do you agree, why or why not?

- Can you think of a time your "temperature" changed the attitude of your wife and children? Looking back, what do you think that says about your role as the leader of your home?

- Whom do you know who expresses a strong confidence in the goodness of God?

- How is the biblical relationship between thoughts and actions and emotions different than how the world connects them?

- What is one way Christian men can put "right thoughts lead to right actions lead to right feelings" into practice in their homes?

- Cheerfulness of heart is not talked about very much anymore. How can having a cheerful heart be a blessing to you and those around you?

Your Ministry
. . . .

(1) Practice Loving Discretion

- How is practicing loving discretion a form of being your wife's protector?
- Why might it be unwise for a wife to tell specific details of another woman's situation to her husband?
- Have you ever told someone something in confidence and that person told someone else? What did you think about what he or she did?
- How can being a deep well be a form of serving someone?
- How are being a deep well for someone to confide in and being a burden-lifter related?
- Read Psalm 103:12, Micah 7:19, and James 5:16. How can being a good, confidential listener be a burden-lifting ministry to others?

(2) Don't Neglect your Family for Ministry

- Pastor Paul Dean said, "If Satan wants to destroy a culture, he attacks the family." What are some examples of this you are seeing in your own culture?
- What are some ways a man can sin in sacrificing his wife and family for ministry?
- Do you think you do a good job balancing family and ministry? Discuss with your wife; what does she think?
- Who are men you have looked up to in ministry? Were you able to spend time in their homes? If so, what did you observe about their homes? Did they reflect Jesus?
- In what ways can a Christian man look to Jesus as his role model for balancing home and ministry?

(3) Take Control of Your Time and Your Commitments

- What did John Calvin mean when he said, "The heart is an idol factory"? Have you seen that in your own heart?

- Read Mark 8:36. How can a Christian man apply that verse to his work and his Christian service?

- Is your culture a time-oriented culture that relies on calendars and appointments? If so, how do you guard against your calendar being full of too many commitments?

- Do you think you are good at saying no? If you are pressured to say yes, do you tend to give in, or do you stand your ground?

- If you are married, talk to your wife about the amount of time and attention you give her. Does she think it's a good balance? How about the time you make for your children?

(4) Get Wisdom for Life-Changing Decisions

- Explain the following statement from Dr. Scott in your own words, as if you were discussing it with a Christian friend: "The knowledge of God leads to the fear of God, which leads to loving God, which leads to loving others."
- What is the relationship between having a fear of the Lord and getting wisdom?
- How does biblical wisdom make decision-making easier?
- Have you ever had a time where you decided to go in one direction and the Lord providentially redirected you in another one? What happened?
- We know the Lord is sovereign and that He controls everything. How can trusting in God's sovereignty over the affairs of your life give you peace, comfort, and confidence about decisions you make?

About Anthony Russo

For twenty years Anthony Russo was a nominal cultural Christian. That is, until September 2005 when the Lord soundly saved him. "I really am what the Bible calls 'born again.' I'm not who I was, my life and my heart are completely different. Selfishness, guilt, and shame were replaced with a genuine love for God and people. Jesus changed my life. He can change yours, too."

Since then Anthony has wanted to tell the world about Jesus. He is the author of several 30-day devotionals for *Anchor*, the devotional ministry of Haven Today, numerous blog articles, and the book *Jesus Changed Everything: He Changed History, He Can Change Your Story*.

Anthony Russo is the creator and, along with his wife, Amy, co-host of the weekly

Christian podcast, Grace and Peace Radio, available on your favorite podcast app, The Christian Podcast Community, or at GraceandPeaceRadio.com.

Anthony has an MA in Biblical Counseling and a Master of Divinity from Luther Rice College and Seminary. He and Amy live in Greenville, South Carolina

Made in the USA
Columbia, SC
23 May 2024

35655709R00057